Susie Montgomery Best

The Fallen Pillar Saint

Susie Montgomery Best

The Fallen Pillar Saint

ISBN/EAN: 9783337337421

Printed in Europe, USA, Canada, Australia, Japan

Cover: Foto ©Lupo / pixelio.de

More available books at **www.hansebooks.com**

THE
Fallen Pillar Saint

AND OTHER POEMS.

BY
SUSIE M. BEST.

NEW YORK:
G. W. Dillingham, Publisher,
Successor to G. W. Carleton & Co.
MDCCCXC.

COPYRIGHT, 1889,
BY
SUSIE M, BEST.

CONTENTS.

	Page
The Fallen Pillar Saint	5
After Dissolution	11
The Infinite	14
Love is Aweary!	16
Lamia	18
In Time of Winter Winds	24
Love is not Tempted!	25
America!	26
The Wooing of Adonis	27
"Ich Habe Gelebt Und Geliebt."	29
Herein is Love	30
In Fairy Land	31
Cloyment	32
The Song of the Night-wind	33
Who is the Happy Man?	34
The Common Fate	36
Desolation	37
A Problem	38
The Ideal	39
Dormant	40
Theseus' Plea	41
What Lies Beyond?	42
Let me not Forget Thee	44
The Old Year	45
Saint or Siren?	46
Faustine	48
The Poet	50
Food for Laughter	51
Slumber Song	52
Wee Thing, Sweet Thing	53
Galatea	54
The Year and June	55
World-Hardened	57
The Years and I	58
The Poet's Scorn	59
The Little Woman	60
A Misconception	61
Gladys	62
The Pessimist's View	63
Eventide	65

Contents.

	Page
The World's Delusions	66
Under the Sod	67
The Curse of Rank	68
A Song of Dreams	71
The Rush of the Times	72
Farewell	74
The Story of a Soul	76
Baby.	79
Paolo to Francesca	80
Across the Crowd	81
Dead	82
Yearning	84
Sweetheart	85
Progress	86
Hide Frae the World!	91
When the Fierce Fates Frown!	92
My Laddie	93
Parted	94
Sae Ill the Day!	95
The Chimla-Lug	96
The Bairns	97
Scotch Song	98
Alane	99
Mirandy	100
Wrapped up in Literatoor	102
Invocation to Time	105
Happy	105
Cover the Embers!	106
Break in the Circle	106
Only a Memory	107
Thus it is	107
June	108
Love's Sanctity	109
Lullbaye	109
Thou and I	110
Sunset	110
Echoes	111
Liberty	111
The Voiceless	112
Yea!	113
Sirius	114
Shadowed	115
First and Last	116
Sweet Yesterday	116
Bitter Sweet	117
The Daisy	118
Lo! When the Moon	119
The Heritage	119
The Crowning of Genius	120

POEMS.

THE FALLEN PILLAR SAINT.

A pillar saint was I, a pillar saint,
As free well-nigh as angels from the taint
Of earthly sin and shame. And night and day
For years did I beat on my breast and pray,
And wrestle with the Lord that he would keep
Me pure and undefiled—yea, I did heap
My pleadings high as is His great white throne,
And at my life no man could cast a stone
Until *she* came. O woman, what a curse
Art thou! than ravenous lions worse, far worse,
And wily thou as sleek, insidious snake,
That, carrying deep damnation in its wake,
Doth still beguile, and with false lying charm
Lure, like the will-o'-wisp, to deadly harm!
O woman, woman, thou it is that hast
Undone me, and made all my righteous past
A ridicule and mocking farce for men,
And hurled me where I ne'er can rise again!

And yet, when I remember that fierce fire
That burned my soul to passionate desire,
And turned each fibre to a thrilling nerve,
I marvel that I did not sooner swerve.
She came to beg my interceding prayer!
The liar! 'twas to tempt me! All her hair,
Long as herself, was from her hood unbound,
And wrapped her like a golden glory round,
A mist of radiant light, and thro' its sheen
The gleaming whiteness of her robes was seen.
Her supple limbs, her lissome form were part
Revealed, and I the beating of her heart
Could see beneath the folds of gold where lay
Her swelling breasts. Ah, God! what charms were they!
And she did kneel low at my pillar's base,
Did upward turn the magic of her face,
And did in meek and reverent tones implore
That I, the saint, would lay her name before
The Lord, for she so great a sinner was
That mightily she feared to plead her cause
Without my prayer. Ah, when, my God, did I
Such fervent penitence hear in a cry?
Her marble hands all meekly did she raise
In supplication. Thus for days and days
She seemingly did agonize in prayer,
Nor wearied not, but ever lingered there.
And she did ofttimes beat her breast and cry,
"He will not bless—too vile, too vile am I!"
And night and night came she robed in her hair,
As tho' she were a bird caught in a snare
Of gold. And she did say to me, "O saint,
Thou pillar saint, my heart doth wax all faint
Of faith. Why is't thy word doth not avail
With Him?" (Thus she, all fair, and sweet, and pale.)
"Come down," she saith, "from off thy pillar, oh,

Thou saint. Mayhap I may some healing know
If I but touch thee once. Yea, I am sure
Thy holy hand my doubting fears can cure.
O come thou down, thou saint, deny not me,
O come and bring thy healing powers with thee!"
And thus she did beguile me with her tongue,
And I, as tho' some siren voice had sung
To me, did get me from my pillar's height
To where she knelt to me in piteous plight,
And she did bend her head and kiss my feet.
(Ah! at her touch an unknown feverish heat
Shot through my veins!) And she did beg that I
Would tell her all that I endured on my
Lone pillar since I was a saint. And she
Did say that no man had the fame of me
In any land. And I, pleased at her word,
(Alas! how easy vanity is stirred!)
Did tell her of the many bitter nights
I had spent there, all barren of delights,
And how I did endure the frost and heat
Alike, and how I braved the winter's sleet
And glaring summer sun uncovered all,
And pangs of pain and passion would appall
Her tender soul. At which she nearer drew,
So near that on my face her hot breath blew,
And she did say, " Ah, surely such an one
Could *now* do any sin nor be undone!"
And she did look on me with loving eye,
Did lean her lips upon my hand and sigh,
" Ah, what a man art thou! Alas that thou
Shouldst be a saint! Alas!" whereat my brow
Grew hot as tho' a furnace blast did blow
It o'er, and in my veins a fire did flow
In place of blood. Some subtle sorcery
Did then and there assail and master me,

My reason fled, and I did open wide
My arms, did crush her beauty 'gainst my side,
I did forget me then both Heaven and earth,
And naught did seem to me of any worth
But this one woman's beauteous face. And she
Did nestle in my bosom happily,
Did coo in silver tones: "Ah, now thou art
A *man!* I know it by thy beating heart
That throbs against my own." And she did take
My hand, and on her breast, white as a flake
Of snow, did press it hard, and she her lips
Did lay on mine—did draw long bee-like sips
Of bliss thro' them. Those lips! No language serves
That can describe their tempting luscious curves!
Each separate time I met them I did feel
A sweet delicious fire throughout me steal;
Each strainéd fibre thrilled with fierce delight,
A mist of ecstacy swept o'er my sight,
And in my ears there came a rushing sound,
As I were in a sea and being drowned;
The soul crept from my body and did float
Away to Heaven itself in Passion's boat!
No thought took I of place, nor circumstance,
Nor time, in that divine, delirious trance;
No rapture else could earth or Heaven bestow,
No keener joy could saint or seraph know,
Than thrilled throughout my being, when her kiss
Roused in my bosom such a maddening bliss!
Then she did point her hand in laughing scorn
Upon the pillar where both night and morn
I had my weary, wrestling vigils kept,
And she from out my arms an instant stept,
And flung from her the mantle of her hair,
And stood in her voluptuous beauty fair.
And spread her arms and said to me: "Wilt there

The Fallen Pillar Saint.

Upon thy pillar, saint? or here, here where
My heart doth beat for thee?" And I, ah I,
Did catch her to me with a quick drawn sigh,
Did glue my lips to hers, and in my arms
Did crush her and the wealth of her fair charms.
And she did lead me from the place to dwell
With her in a most blissful Heavenly Hell,
And more and more did she seduce my heart,
Until I could not live from her apart.
And tho' I knew that in the world did all
Spit on my name and ridicule my fall,
And hold me up in mocking scorn for aye,
Still did I linger in her curséd sway.
And she, when she did have me all undone,
Did on a sudden my embraces shun,
Did thrust me violently from her side,
And from the reach of my stretched arms did glide,
Did point her hand at me in scorn ! in scorn !
Did say : "*And thou art he*—he who hath worn
The name of *Saint!* whom no flesh could seduce,
Nor could his chains of righteousness unloose !
Thou, he, who all temptation did defy,
Did set himself upon a pillar high,
Did say that none could draw him to the earth !
Ah ! better, better, hadst thou ne'er had birth,
For thou art but a woman's fool to-day !
I did deceive thee, saint,—*a woman's way*—
I vowed that thou shouldst be a man for me ;
That I would wreck thy saintly soul for thee,
And make thee pant and pine as others do,
And now, that done, my use of thee is through !
Farewell, O fool, farewell !" With that did she,
That curséd sorceress, depart from me ;
And I, I do bethink me, I did fall
Upon the ground like dead, and thus thro' all

The night did I lie there; but when the sun
Did rise, I, crying out, "Undone ! undone !"
Did turn me from the place like one gone mad,
Did get me in despair to where I had,
In days long gone, lived on my pillar high,
And there did this inscription meet my eye :
"*The pillar of a fallen saint behold!*"
No more, no less, but, oh, the pain that rolled
Across my soul like some great stormy ocean,
When I remembered all my lost devotion !
Ah, I did kneel me down low at the base
Of that my pillar ; I did curse the face
That had beguiled me from stern virtue's path,
And brought on me the mocking and the wrath
Of all, and did condemn my soul to burn
In Hell, for ne'er, I feel it, can I earn
Forgiveness for my sin—the deadly taint
Hath cursed for aye *the fallen pillar saint!*

AFTER DISSOLUTION.

Lo ! after dissolution,
   In the Hall of Judgment, I,
Before the Ruler pleading
   That the soul of me might die !
" Behold," my spirit sayeth,
   " Give me a choice to-day,
I did not crave existence,
   Why should I live alway ?
Life, it was thrust upon me,
   It was no wish of mine,
In all my years of living
   Woe was my only wine.
I slept beneath the nightshade,
   I drank its deadly dew,
I buffeted the whirlwinds,
   I pain and passion knew.
And now I see before me
   A myriad other lives,
Throughout eternal ages
   The vital spark survives.
And O, my spirit shrinketh,
   It sees both gain and loss,
But the crown that it may gather
   Seems scarcely worth the cross.
I am not strong to suffer,
   I fear the tears of blood,
I pray for solemn stillness,
   I beg Oblivion's flood."

Lo! after dissolution,
  In the Hall of Judgment, I,
Thus pleading to the Ruler,
  Thus answered He my sigh:
"True, life is not election
  And birth an unsought gift,
But after death the spirit
  The blind constraint may lift.
No soul need live forever,
  Before it lie two ways,
To sink into a Lethe
  Or live eternal days.
Now, ponder well, O spirit,
  Before thy choice is made;
Look thou on both conditions—,
  Nor be thou sore afraid."

Lo! after dissolution,
  In the Hall of Judgment, I,
Aweighing in the balance
  To live alway or die!
Spread out before my vision
  An endless length of days,
An ever climbing upward
  Thro' sunlight and thro' haze.
New lives, new loves, new passions,
  New aims, new hopes, new fears,
New victories, new torments,
  Throughout undying years.
An ever toiling onward
  Thro' mingled love and hate,
While souls are spurred to glory
  And worlds roll on to fate!

After Dissolution.

Lo! after dissolution,
   I pondering on this,
On life and all life's burdens,
   On life and all life's bliss.
Spread out before my vision
   A stirless, slumbering sea,
Where never wave nor billow
   Breathe what in it may be.
A vasty solemn stillness,
   A passionless deep calm,
A freedom from all yearning,
   No sorrow, neither balm.
Impenetrable darkness,
   A gulf where all is lost,
Soul-sense and spirit-striving,
   Attainèd hopes and crost.
The wondrous Sea of Silence,
   Oblivious retreat,
Where the soul that wills may perish,
   To forgetfulness complete!

Lo! after dissolution,
   In the Hall of Judgment, I,
In the presence of the Ruler,
   Electing there—to die!

THE INFINITE.

Thro' vaulted vastnesses, by longing lit,
We see the shadow of the infinite !
The thund'rings of Eternity on Time
Ring in our ears like some majestic rhyme
                Struck from a soul sublime !

But, oh ! this reaching for the infinite,
This restiveness of soul beneath the bit
And bridle of the flesh !   This yearning of
The spirit for the sunlit space above—
                For everlasting love !

Alas ! to ever on life's outskirts sit
And only vaguely grasp the infinite !
To feel the flutterings of immortal wings
Held by the bonds of many sordid strings
                From spiritual wanderings !

Is there no mode but Death whereby to quit
Life's limitations for the infinite ?
May we not by desire intense propel
Our vision to those fields of asphodel
                Where saints seraphic dwell ?

Nay ! earth makes us insentient and unfit
The infiltration of the infinite
To bear.   The still white glory of that sphere
Would blast us did our world-sight see it clear
                Within Time's cincture here.

The Infinite.

Humanity is of too gross a grit
The consecration of the infinite
To comprehend.   Till supersenuous sight
Be ours, the revelation will be slight
                Of Infinite Delight.

LOVE IS AWEARY!

Ripe red lips? What of them, he saith,
With their curling corners and sweet-blown breath?—
They kindle no more the dead desire,
Nor rouse the flame of amorous fire,
Sweeter dull sleep than their kisses—and shyer.
     Love is aweary!

Wide, love-drenched eyes! What witchcraft they
The masters of could rouse to play
The languorous languor of lulled delight?
Passion-swept eyes grow tame and trite,
Love tires of such in a day and a night.
     Love is aweary!

Smooth, lithe limbs, delicious breasts,
Softer than Spring birds' down-lined nests?
O yea! and yea! but these lose power,
Love is a frail anemone flower
The wild wind blasts in an untoward hour.
     Love is aweary!

Maddening beauties but half concealed,
More luring far than the full revealed,
Woman's sorcery and winsome wile,
Clinging hand and enticing smile?
But these things cloy and cease to beguile.
     Love is aweary!

Love is Aweary!

Songs as sweet as the vesper chimes,
Haunting the soul like a poet's rhymes,
Picturing joys with their subtle breath?
Impotent—impotent *all* he saith,
The pyre of passion has burned to death.
     Love is aweary!

Perfumed hair like the softest silk,
Crowning a brow as white as milk,
Veins with a molten fire aglow?
These are but common wares, and low,
They stem not Repletion's sluggish flow.
     Love is aweary!

LAMIA.

I.

Was once upon a time a maid most wondrous fair,
Like unto sunshine kissing gold, her silken hair,
And yet each waving tendril someway did suggest
The picture of a writhing serpent ill at rest.
Pale green her eyes, like unto emeralds in the sun ;
Cold eyes that evermore reluctant homage won,
The while one gazèd in their depths there seemed to swim
Before his sight a mighty forest, dark and dim,
Of lordly trees close-laced with heavy underbrush
And overhanging vines and grasses long and lush ;
And thro' its shades a sullen river seemed to glide
All fearfully, as tho' some guilty sin 'twould hide,
And far adown the vasty aisles of silence, he
A slimy sinuous snake evanishing would see,
At which with shuddering horror he would turn, when, lo!
All'd vanish in the air, e'en as a mist I trow ;
And when he'd rouse him from the nightmare of his fright,
He would but see the lovely maid all gold and white !

II.

A prince there dwelt within a mighty city's gate
Had newly wedded him a wife of great estate,
The apple of his eye was she, fair as the morn,
And like a grand young goddess in her holy scorn

Of vain deceits, impostures and vile treacheries,
Nor ever in her soul was room for sins like these.
And he—the prince—her new-made husband did adore
Her very name, yea, he did set her e'en before
His God within his heart so deep his passion was,
And ofttimes midst the duties of the day he'd pause
And ponder on the blessedness divine was his
In calling wife, a woman glorious as this!

III.

But, lo! how Fate doth find us each and every one!
The highest nor the lowliest beneath the sun
Can e'er escape the mastering hand of Destiny,
In turn each to that conqueror must subject be.

IV

These twain made one, did on a time as lovers will,
Betake them from the jarring crowd and wandered, till
They came unto a spot where they could be alone,
And there, with arms enwreathèd and with fond lips grown
In one, they drank them deep of love's divine delights,
And did forget the world and all in passion's flights;
But soft—what form is this comes stealing nigh the bower
Where these, the wedded lovers, stole such a perfect hour;
What long lithe willowy shape with gliding step comes near
And pauses for an instant on the threshold here?
'Tis she—the wondrous maiden of the emerald eyes,—
She set those orbs upon the prince as on a prize

She long had sought—she waved her hand thrice in the air
And strove to weave a nameless spell about the pair.
But half did she succeed—the lily purity
Within the young wife's soul, kept her exempt and free.
But he, the prince, lo, he did lift his eyes and gaze
Into those green, green orbs, and o'er him came a haze.
And as he looked, behold! a forest dark and dim
Spread suddenly before the spell-bound sight of him.
And lo! a guilty river ran in silence there
As tho' it knew of horrid things it did not dare
To tell; and far adown the lonely isles of dread
He saw a writhing serpent rear its spiteful head!
At which, he, with a shuddering horror, turned in fear,
When lo! nought but the wondrous maiden did appear!
Thrice slowly did she wave her hand and then upon
Her lips she set it as a seal—turned, and was gone!
Then rose the wife with sudden anger in her breast,
A strange foreboding sense of ill; upon her pressed
A feeling like to one who every hope has lost,
Whose life by strange disasters, storms and shades is crossed,
And closely clung she to her husband's arm and said,
"Come, love, and let us leave this place of fear and dread,
And get us to our own dear home nor ever think
Of this strange maid. I feel as tho' upon the brink
Of sin and shame we for an instant stood. I fear
To longer linger in this tainted atmosphere."
Like unto one that moves him in a dream he rose,
And let her lead him from the spot nor spoke of those
Green eyes, and yet they were the only things he saw,
Henceforth they were his only will, his only law!

V.

That night, when closely to his breast her head she laid,
He tossed uneasily and thought him of the maid
Whose emerald eyes did seem to draw him even then
Into a forest deep, away from haunts of men :
Whose waving hand did seem to lure him on and on
So strongly that he rose and did his clothing don,
And muttered in his beard, " Within the wood she waits,
She waits for me ! I must beyond the city's gates,
And hie me to her haunts before the morn appears !"
Sleep on, O lily wife, thou'lt wake to woe and tears,
Sleep on and well for thee if thou should'st wake no more,
For all the blessedness of life for thee is o'er,
For see,—like unto one held in a subtle spell
He stealthily doth steal him from thy side to dwell
With her, the wondrous maiden of the emerald eyes,
Forgetful all of thee, and of thy holy ties.
Sleep on—thy last sweet sleep of dear untroubled rest.
Sleep on forever, for thou'lt find that death is best !

VI.

Away beyond the city's gate he hurried him,
Away into the mighty forest, dark and dim,
Of lordly trees and lonely silences and where
She seemed to beckon him, the maid of waving hair,
The curling gold of which did ever bring to mind
The thought of writhing serpents round a tree entwined !
There where the guilty river ran in silent shame
He saw her standing when into the shade he came ;
Thrice did she wave her hand, and drew him nearer still
And bade him come to her and drink of love his fill !

Within the circle of her arms he slowly drew
The charmèd circle; stretched his hand and close unto
His breast he drew her then, and to her lips his own
Were pressed in such a kiss as he had never known.
A kiss that roused a fiery torment in his breast.
But, lo! e'en as he would again have closely pressed
Her ripe red mouth, a sudden horror came o'er him,
The whole broad forest round about him seemed to swim,
The long white arms enwreathed about him seemed to crush
The life out of his heart there in the silent hush;
He struggled to be free, he strove to cast them off,
But their relentless clasp he had no power to doff.
With fearful terror then he raised up cry on cry,
And thro' the woodland did but hear the echoes fly.
Then closèd he his eyes and prayed no more to wake,
For wreathèd round him was no maiden but a snake,
Long, lithe and sinuous, with venomous greedy fangs
Outreaching for his heart, to deal him death's last pangs!

VII.

Behold now, in the morning, when the wife awoke
And found him gone, the heart within her bosom broke,
For straightway with a sudden inspiration she
Did understand that to the maiden he did flee,
And in her heart she did remember how those eyes,
Grass green and cold, were set on him as on a prize
They long had sought, and much she feared some ill to him
Had come, and so she bade her guardsmen search the dim
And mighty forest thro' and thro', if haply they
Might find some trace of him before the close of day.
Then, at her word, into the forest's shade there went
A mighty host, and she in grief's abandonment

Went too, and lo! when in the thickest shade they came,
Near where the guilty river ran in silent shame,
There lying in the woodland space a form they saw
That Death's grim hand had late exempted from earth's
    law,
And far adown the lonely aisles they saw *A Thing*,
A slimy sinuous Snake in haste evanishing !

IN TIME OF WINTER WINDS!

What time the wintry winds 'gan blowing,
    'Gan blowing swift and strong,
Came soft as sounds of crystal snowing,
    Word from the heavenly throng
To one who heard with heart a-glowing,
    The call from earth's rude wrong.

What time the wintry winds 'gan blowing,
    'Gan blowing sad and shrill,
Sat we with tear-blind eyes a-sewing
    Seams for one white and still,
With desolated hearts well knowing
    A corpse the folds would fill!

What time the wintry winds 'gan blowing,
    'Gan blowing late and loud,
Heard we the grave-men clods a-throwing
    On one wound in a shroud,
And from our lives felt gladness going
    Fast in a flying cloud

LOVE IS NOT TEMPTED!

Trailing robes of the richest dye,
Most splendid jewels that gold can buy,
Loveliness decked in marvellous hues?
Love beholds in these but a ruse.
    Love is not tempted!

Fragrance and flowers and voluptuous dance,
And sweet enticements that charms enhance?
These but rouse passion as fleeting as false.
Love wears an armor 'gainst such assaults
    Love is not tempted!

Fiery longings and vows of love
With the sweet caresses and kisses thereof,
Words of worship and songs of praise?
These cannot fix love's wavering gaze.
    Love is not tempted!

Beauty allures not love, nor wealth,
Nor gorgeous trappings, nor youth, nor health;
'Tis that strange elusive thing the soul
Is the only charm can love control.
    Love is not tempted!

AMERICA!

On the highest round of fame you stand,
      America! America!
Peace and plenty in each fair hand,
Your children a loyal close-knit band,
Ready to die for their loved land.
      America! America!

Queen of the nations, old and new,
      America! America!
The eyes of the world are fixed on you!
Keep to your course then, firm and true,
And the God of Israel carry you through.
      America! America!

"Freedom" your watchword and "right" your cry,
      America! America!
Treason and wrong slink shame-faced by,
Cowed by the glance of your eagle eye;
To shake your throne they no longer try,
      America! America!

No shadow of shame your escutcheon mar,
      America! America!
Shine in God's firmament like a star,
Whose glorious gleams reflected are
From millions of worlds anear and afar.
      America! America!

THE WOOING OF ADONIS.

Venus am I; Venus, the fairest of the fair,
The toast of gods, yet am I in despair! despair!
For I have set my heart upon the love of one
Who ever at my near approach will laugh and run!
In all the world there is no sweeter thing than love;
Mere mortals know no greater good, nor gods above!
Adonis, thou fair boy, come hither now and let
Me rouse thee to a passion thou wilt ne'er forget.
But look upon me, am I not divinely fair?
Behold the riotous luxuriance of my hair,
Deep, glossy gold, shot thro' and thro' with fiery red,
The splendid amber aureola of my head!
Come, bury thou thy boy's hands in it amorously
And we will call them white boats in a yellow sea!
Look in my eyes, are they not deeper than the seas,
And bluer than the skies, and full of witcheries?
Is not my cheek a marvel of rose-bloom and snow,
Pale in thy absence, in thy presence all aglow?
Didst e'er see richer, more voluptuous lips than mine?
Come, love, and grow thou drunken deep upon their wine.
Let me but kiss thee, and thou'lt swear the sweetest death
That thou couldst die, would be to let me suck thy breath.
Nay, nay, turn not aside thy head, but rather rest
It here upon the tender blossom of my breast.
I am far fairer than the foam from which I rose;
My breath is sweeter than the sweetest breeze that blows.

Adonis, I am queen! but ever slave to thee,
Adonis, fair Adonis! hearken thou to me.
Come, sweet, and nest within my long, lithe, loving arms,
And list the while I whisper thee of other charms!
What, now! thou wilt not? Oh, alas! alas! that I,
Venus, the queen of love, for love denied should die!

"ICH HABE GELEBT UND GELIEBT."

Enough of song—one's ears wax dull
With too much tune. Let silence lull
Us into peace. We are too sad
To care for mournful airs or glad,
We crave but stillness vast and strong,
We're weary now—enough of song.

Enough of love—it tires the heart,
It poisons with its painful dart ;
One sickens of the sweets it brings,
For they but cover serpent stings
The balm of heaven can scarce remove,
We're weary now—enough of love.

Enough of work—what profits toil ?
The Fates our best endeavors foil ;
'Tis useless climbing up the height,
And useless battling for the right
When hidden foes in ambush lurk,
We're weary now—enough of work.

Enough of life—we cry enough,
The elements have been too rough,
Our ships at sea have all been wrecked,
The waves of time with tears are flecked,
Give us cessation of this strife,
We're weary now—enough of life.

HEREIN IS LOVE.

Herein is love : to take this strange sweet thing
That we call life, and for love's sake to fling
It to that outer darkness men deem death,
That love may have a longer, sweeter breath ;
To face with unaffrighted heart the gloom,
The terror and the agony of doom.

Herein is love : to lift another's cross,
To give away the gold and keep the dross,
To trample into dust the worm of self,
To crowd its clam'rings on the soul's back shelf
Nor let it ever dare upraise its head,
Deny its every call till it lies dead.

Herein is love : to strip the shoulders bare,
If need be, that a frailer one may wear
A mantle to protect it from the storm,
To bear the frost-king's breath so one be warm ;
To crush the tears it would be sweet to shed,
And smile so others may have joy instead.

Herein is love : to daily sacrifice
The hope that to the bosom closest lies,
To mutely bear reproach and suffer wrong,
Nor lift the voice to show where both belong,
Nay, now, nor tell it e'en to God above—
Herein is love, indeed, herein is love.

IN FAIRY LAND.

In fairy land, in fairy land,
The rivers run o'er golden sand ;
The drops of dew are pearls for you,
The skies are ever cloudless blue.

In fairy land, in fairy land,
Do love and law walk hand in hand ;
No bitter tears, nor broken years,
Nor fragmentary wreck appears.

In fairy land, in fairy land,
Hearts never fail nor high hopes strand ;
No graves are there, no unheard prayer,
No ghosts of joys that once were fair.

In fairy land, in fairy land,
Fruition's sweet as it was planned ;
Fate's fatal wand can wound nor brand,
Ah me ! ah me ! in fairy land !

CLOYMENT.

What matters bright hair of the sun's own gold,
Or a balmy breast of a beauteous mold
When desire is dead and the heart is cold?

What matters the sorcery of subtle sighs,
Or the swimming sweetness of slumbrous eyes
When the winds of longing no longer rise?

What matters a cheek of a peach-like bloom,
Or a breath like the violet's faint perfume
When love is but wormy dust in his tomb?

What matters a face like the Morning Star,
Or brows like the brows of the high gods are
When the eyes of passion are set afar?

What matters a beauty beyond compare,
Or white hands clasped in a pleading prayer
When love is tired and does not care?

The undulant grace of a perfect form
Cannot serve to keep the pulses warm
When Satiety takes the sense by storm.

Beauty has never a spell to cast,
Can hold the wavering fealty fast
When the surfeited soul recoils at last.

The emollient sweet of a lingering kiss
Has no power to charge the heart with bliss
When Cloyment deadens Delight, I wis.

THE SONG OF THE NIGHT-WIND.

The night-wind is singing a song, a song !
Ho ! Ho ! Ha ! Ha ! for the night-wind's song !
He's wailing in sorrow, he's shrieking in glee,
He's calling the fairies to waltz on the lea,
He's wooing the mermaids to come from their cave
And sport in the moonlight and dance on the wave
He's trilling as soft and as sweet as a bird,
He's telling of love with never a word,
He's whispering low to the dead on the hill,
He taunts them with lying so white and so still ;
He's screaming to eagles in aeries on high,
He dares them came forth and join in his cry,
He's telling them of the wild haunts he has seen,
The fathomless gorges in which he has been,
And how he arose on lightning-like wings,
And saw in the Heavens ineffable things.
He's mourning o'er roses that droop in the hedges,
He's weeping and sobbing o'er dead, withered sedges.
He goes where he wills and he sings as he pleases,
He charms and he soothes and he taunts and he teases .
One moment he's merry, another he's sad,
Now peacefully crooning, now roaring and mad.
O a marvellous song is the night-wind's song !
Ho ! Ho ! Ha ! Ha ! for the night-wind's song !

WHO IS THE HAPPY MAN?

    Who is the happy man?
He whose songs the whole world sings,
Whose words are like to pearls on strings
Of golden thought? Whose fancies ride
High as the stars and there abide,
Who hears the strains of Nature's choir,
And to that music tunes his lyre,
    Is he the happy man?

Not he! not he! for the poet sees
With passionate pains and agonies
The unsung song that is so sublime,
On the luring heights that he cannot climb!

    Who is the happy man?
The lover who has won his maid,
Who unrebuked has ofttimes laid
Upon her lips love's full fond kiss,
And felt her with responsive bliss
Thrill at his touch, and seen her eyes
Grow humid with her ecstacies?
    Is he the happy man?

Not he! not he! for the lover's grief
Is his certainty that bliss is brief;
He knows that his raptures cannot last,
And he shrinks from the cloyment coming fast!

Who is the Happy Man?

  Who is the happy man?
He whom his latter days have found
In the place of power,—sceptred, crowned?
Whose word is law and whose wish a wand
Controlling at will a mighty land;
Who ever hears the applauding crowd
Proclaiming him king and chief aloud?
  Is he the happy man?

Not he! not he! for the so-called great
Are slaves of the mightier power—Fate—
And the crown they wear and the wand they wield
To the monarch Death must sometime yield!

  Who is the happy man?
He who has delved in Nature's deeps,
And read of the secrets that she keeps
From common eyes? Whose awe-struck gaze
Has lighted on some of her hidden ways?
Who has broadened his view till he sees as far
As the faintest, fartherest fixèd star?
  Is he the happy man?

Not he! not he! for the Sphinx of "Why"
Is ever before his eager eye,
And he fails to find in the spheres that roll
The craved Eldorado of the soul!

  There is no happy man!
The name of happiness is all
That the boldest mortal e'er can call
His own. The substance is so fine,
So subtly nice and so divine,
That but its shadow blesses him,
And oh, the shadow is so dim!
  There is no happy man!

THE COMMON FATE.

The roses of June-time decay,
In a night they wither away!
The winds of the morn,
With a half-tender scorn,
Bear on their pinions the ashes forlorn.

The sweet forest songsters grow still,
In an hour they forget their glad trill;
The bleak winter breath
In the woods wandereth,
And lo! the birdlings are chilled unto death!

The glad babbling brooklets run dry,
They faint in the glare of July,
The sun's burning heat
With a pitiless beat,
Checks their musically moving feet.

Passionate hearts turn cold,
With the passing of youth they grow old!
The swift falling years
Drench their fire with tears,
Their wine turns to water, their raptures to fears.

DESOLATION.

The dead man in his coffin lay—
(Oh, the patter and drip of the rain!)
The low-hung clouds and the dreary day,
The awesome still of the pulseless form
Unmoved by the wild November storm,
(Oh, the patter and drip of the rain!)
The deathly chill of the brow of snow,
The sobbing notes of the widow's woe,
The sickening scent of the roses strewn
Round face and hands to be hidden soon,
(Oh, the patter and drip of the rain!)
The dull gray light of the dull gray sky,
Dull as the glassy glazèd eye.
The mocking bird whose glad notes gushed,
Now in his cage all strangely hushed.
(Oh, the patter and drip of the rain!)
The strange, weird notes of the wind's refrain,
Like the wailing cry of a soul in pain,
Oh, the dreary and desolate day
When the dead man in his coffin lay.

A PROBLEM.

Love and its rapturous fond delights,
Kisses, caresses, and passionate flights,
Murmurings tender and sweet mad bliss,
Would you? or a heart contented to miss
      All this?

Love means capacity for pain—
At the birth of Passion, Peace is slain,
Sleep and untroubled dreams grow shyer,
Freedom is lost in the flaming fire
      Of Desire.

Weighed in the balance, which were loss—
A loveless life, or love and its cross?
Which were the wiser, the calm repose
Of a stirless heart, or one that knows
      Love's woes?

THE IDEAL.

As valorous as the shepherd lad
   That laid Goliath low,
As stainless as Sir Galahad
   Must be my love, I trow.
And he must rich as Crœsus be,
   And eloquent as Paul,
Fair as Adonis was to see,
   Else I'll not heed his call!

Love great as Jonathan's must move
   The fountains of his heart,
He must as mild as Moses prove,
   In Samson's strength have part.
And patient as the patriarch Job,
   And free from any sin—
You say there's none such on the globe?
   Then none my love will win!

DORMANT.

Sweet, with your red wet lips, and eyes
Where a powerful passion dormant lies,
Will the spell that holds you calm be broken
When my fiery words of love are spoken?

Sweet, I would barter heaven for this,
To be in your arms, and feel your kiss
Drawing my soul thro' my ravished lips,
As the whirlpool swallows the fated ships.

Sweet, I would wreck my life to rest
On the molded argent of your breast,
To feel your beautiful satin skin
Grow warm with the fire that burned within.

Sweet, I would willingly die to know
My touch made your pulses faster go,
To think that your fair young body thrilled
With love and longing as my soul willed.

Sweet, I would face the world's disdain,
Yea, I would count its scorn a gain,
Could I toy with that glory of red-gold hair,
And be enchained in its silken snare.

Sweet, I would brave eternal fire
To reach the summit of my desire;
To drift together to Love's bright sea,
And know it was sweet to you as to me.

THESEUS' PLEA.

My Ariadne I did leave,
Yea, tho' I knew that she would grieve;
    But could I stay?
    Love had turned gray,
I had but ashes left to give,
The fire of love refused to live,
    Then why delay?

I did grow weary of her eyes,
Impatient of her amorous sighs;
    Her kisses cloyed,
    Her touch annoyed,
She was a drag upon my life—
(Thus many a man finds many a wife
    When love grows void!)

I could not help it that love died—
Could I his corpse chain to my side?
    Could I still smile
    And her beguile
Into the dream she yet was dear?
Nay, kinder 'twas to disappear,
    And far less vile!

WHAT LIES BEYOND?

Darkness eternal?
Splendor supernal?
Suff'ring infernal?
    What lies beyond?

What bells can peal it?
What power unseal it?
What seer reveal it?
    What lies beyond?

Winds wailing o'er us,
In solemn chorus,
What is before us?
    What lies beyond?

Sea surging under
Do thy waves thunder
Of Unknown Wonder?
    What lies beyond?

Meteors flying
From stars a-sighing,
Know ye ere dying
    What lies beyond?

Sun of fierce splendor,
Pale Luna tender,
Can ye surrender
    What lies beyond?

What Lies Beyond?

Worlds rolling ever
With ceaseless endeavor,
Can ye tell never
    What lies beyond?

Weird willows weeping,
Green ivy creeping
Where graves are sleeping,
    What lies beyond?

World-famous sages,
Found ye on pages
Of long-buried ages
    What lies beyond?

Prophet or poet,
Can either show it,
Do either know it,
    What lies beyond?

Soul in us burning,
Spirit-sense yearning,
Earth-passions spurning
    What lies beyond

Darkness eternal?
Splendor supernal?
Suff'ring infernal?
    What lies beyond?

LET ME NOT FORGET THEE.

Lord, let me not forget Thee
   When my richly-laden ships
Sail proudly into harbor,
   When joy is at my lips.

When skies are blue above me,
   And flowers smile at my feet,
Lord, let me not forget Thee
   When life is fresh and sweet.

Lord, let me not forget Thee
   When favoring breezes blow;
When no shadow shuts the sunlight—
   When splendid moons sail low.

Lord, let me not forget Thee
   When love its halo lends,
When in a sky of glory
   Hope's glittering rainbow bends.

I know, I know in sorrow
   I make myself Thy guest;
When lowering storms alarm me
   I hide me in Thy breast.

Therefore I pray Thee, Father,
   To draw my thoughts to Thee,
Nor let my soul forget Thee
   When pleasures rain on me.

THE OLD YEAR.

Dying alone in the midnight drear,
  Sweet year, sad year!
Shall I not sorrow a bit at thy bier,
I to whom thou hast been so dear,
  Sweet year, sad year?

Paling before the New Year's face,
  Loved days, lost days!
Shall I not hymn some notes of praise,
Songs of thanks for flowery ways,
  Loved days, lost days?

Drifting away to the Unknown Sea,
  To Eternity!
Shall I not mourn to part from thee,
Belovèd, whom I shall no more see
  Till Eternity?

Dead—at the stroke of the midnight bell!
  How the echoes swell!
'Tis the angels tolling thy passing knell.
Shall I not weep, "Farewell, farewell!"
  While the echoes swell?

SAINT OR SIREN?

One with luring lips and bewildering eyes
That would thrill a saint in Paradise,
Can turn my blood to a sea of fire,
Whose surging waves roll ever higher.

When with a wild delight I feel
Her passionate arms around me steal,
I lose in the fierce delicious flame
That burns my soul, both honor and shame.

When she lays on my lips the dewy rose
Of her mouth, the madness my bosom knows
Is like some whirlwind's imperious force
That obstacles scatters like chaff from its course.

And when, with a voice like a cooing dove,
She wooingly whispers her words of love,
I yield myself to her sweet caress,
And forget all else in her loveliness!

Another, in whose calm eyes of blue,
The glory of heaven glimmers thro',
Can hush with a saintly glance my sighs,
And quell the flames that from passion rise.

When I meet her rapt angelic gaze
I feel as tho' I stood face to face
With one who had seen the glory of God,
And my restless fever is quenched and awed.

Saint or Siren? 47

At her kiss no electric thrill shoots thro'
My heart, but there rises before my view
A vision of high and holy things,
And I hear the flutter of angels' wings.

At the touch of her cool soft hand, my blood
Grows calm like a spent retreating flood ;
And her voice like a silver bell recalls
My soul from the siren's witching thralls.

Thus in the balance I waver ever,
Unable the soul and the sense to sever ;
Yet some day either will master me,
The saint or the siren, and *which shall it be?*

FAUSTINE.

You are a syren, fair Faustine,
As was Trojan Helen, famous queen;
Your beauty is a wondrous spell
For which a man would brave e'en Hell.
And yet you have no heart, Faustine,
Tho' you *play* you are carved of fire:
'Tis but a bit of art, Faustine,
Your trembling passion is a liar,
   Wily Faustine!

You laugh to think I've found you out;
You little care—few men will doubt
When once you lure them to your arms,
Your beauty deadens doubt's alarms.
Aye, coyly draw your lace aside,
Half bare those drifts of dazzling snow,
Enticing nests where pleasures bide,
Their power to charm full well you know,
   Artful Faustine!

O yea! your arms I know, Faustine,
Can counterfeit a glow, Faustine,
And like a full-blown rose your lips,
From whence a honeyed nectar slips.
Your hair is sweetly riotous—
Wild hair that will not stay in place—
It suits you, Faustine, better thus,
Its fond disorder adds a grace,
   O sly Faustine!

Faustine.

Reign in your triumph insolent,
Allure with every blandishment,
Your matchless beauty gives you power
To sway men like a wind-blown flower;
And this is all your being craves,
To rouse their passions to a flame,
To see them bow infatuate slaves,
And burn at mention of your name,
      Crafty Faustine!

How like a queen you look, Faustine,
Who would no rival brook, Faustine,
And yet it would be better far
To other be than what you are;
How will you show when Time, the Thief,
With stealthy pace steals after you,
And turns you to a withered leaf,
What potent philter can you brew
      'Gainst that, Faustine?

Your lovers will desert you then,
So fickle are the hearts of men
That only fleshly fetters chain,
They traitors turn when beauties wane.
'Twere better, better far, Faustine,
To be a wife, and mother true,
Her charm keeps ever fresh and green
Above ephemera like you,
      Hapless Faustine!

THE POET.

A beautiful realm of illusions is
   The land where the poet lives,
The common things of the common earth,
   His fancy a glory gives.

The eyes of the poet the lenses wear,
   That dwarf all things that are base;
They pierce thro' the murky hazes of time,
   And light on creative grace.

The ear of the poet no discord discerns
   In the symphony old earth plays;
His soul has been tuned to its passionate chords,
   And its clarion notes of praise.

The soul of the poet exultantly wings
   Its way to the portal of heaven;
He waits not till Death, for Eternity's joys
   To him on the earth are given.

The poet's the child of the Universe,
   And the Universe is his throne;
No single orbit confines his soul,
   But every pathway's his own.

FOOD FOR LAUGHTER.

The baby is merry to see her new toy,
She crows and dances in childish joy,
She tastes as much bliss as ever, I wis,
Will be hers in a world as dreary as this.

The maiden is merry to dream of her love,
No fear has she it ever will rove,
And until she sees how swiftly it flees,
She'll not know there's rue as well as heartsease.

The mother is merry to clasp her firstborn,
She smiles to think she was ever forlorn;
The height of her bliss is her baby's kiss,
What happiness think you is equal to this?

The worm he is merry to feed on the dead,
He chuckles each time the death-roll is read,
He gloats in the graves, o'er monarchs and slaves,
No merriment greater than this he craves.

Now which is the merriest think you of these?
Which one has the plaything that longest will please?
Ah, the babe may forget—the maiden regret,
The mother turn cold, but the worm will laugh yet!

SLUMBER SONG.

On the sea of sleep we're sailing,
    Sailing, sailing, sailing!
Mother's love a love unfailing,
Round the baby's bark is trailing,
While upon the sea we're sailing,
    Sailing, sailing, sailing.

See the waves of slumber rolling,
    Rolling, rolling, rolling!
All the evening bells are tolling,
Mother's song her babe's consoling,
While around us waves are rolling,
    Rolling, rolling, rolling!

High upon the waves we're riding,
    Riding, riding, riding!
Now in deeper seas we're gliding,
Sleep is on his lids abiding,
While upon the waves we're riding,
    Riding, riding, riding!

WEE THING, SWEET THING!

O but to feel her lips on mine,
      Wee thing, sweet thing!
O but to drink their 'wildering wine,
      Wee thing, sweet thing!
O but to sun in her radiant smile,
O but to yield to her witching wile,
O but to clasp her close awhile,
      Wee thing, sweet thing!

Hid in the heart of God she is,
      Wee thing, sweet thing!
Heaven is nearer and dearer for this,
      Wee thing, sweet thing!
Oft thro' the gateway of the skies
I catch the lambent fire of her eyes,
And I know that Paradise holds my prize,
      Wee thing, sweet thing!

GALATEA.

Galatea! Galatea,
'Tis Pygmalion calls.
Be a woman, Galatea!
Burst thy marble thralls,
Doff thy cold and pulseless quiet,
Let love's fiery storm
Surging o'er thee like a whirlwind
Thrill thy stony form!

Think but on the sweets of loving,
Think but on its bliss;
Think what dormant worlds of rapture
Waken at a kiss.
Let me teach thee love's endearments
In the tenderest fashion,
Let me see thy pale perfection
All aglow with passion.

Come from off thy stately column,
Cast thy cold repose,
Test with me delicious pleasure
That no surfeit knows.
See—I clasp my arms around thee,
Gods, her silence break!
Let this kiss arouse the statue,
Galatea—awake!

THE YEAR AND JUNE.

The Year came searching for June, one day;
He had grown so weary of pure cold May,
May—that had never waxed fierce with love,
May—that no passionate pleadings could move,

He had wooed her with ardor, and fervor, and fire,
But he roused no touch of kindred desire;
And his love, like all that's repulsed and denied,
Burned low, turned to ashes, and finally died.

Then he took him to thinking of sweet, wild June,
And he caught up his harp and set it in tune;
He curled all his locks and made himself gay,
And eagerly sought for her flower-decked way.

He made him a crown of red roses for her,
His soul with his new born hopes was astir,
In fancy he clasped her warm beauty at will,
And felt her with passion responsively thrill.

He hunted her high, and hunted her low,
With heart all aflame and eyes all aglow;
He found her asleep in a bower of bliss,
And roused her from dreams with a lingering kiss.

She started and blushed with a swift sudden shame,
But he clasped her and held her and low breathed love's
    name;
He kissed her to rapture and soothed away fear,
And made her the beautiful bride of the Year.

And May?—ah, May was forgotten and dead,
June was the queen with the crown on her head.
May was too pure, and too shy, and too cold,
To keep the heart of the Year in her hold.

WORLD-HARDENED.

We do not care that the skies are argent,
   That the hills are a dewy green,
The rose-sweet blooms of the lavish summer
   Blossom well-nigh unseen,
For the weight of our years is upon our spirit,
   And we are world-hardened, I ween.

We do not care for the still, soft splendor
   Circling each rolling sphere,
For the birds that herald the Spring-time's coming
   We do not strain our ear,
For our soul is sunk in a sordid slumber
   And we are world-hardened, I fear.

We do not feel as we felt in childhood,
   Our dreams have not come to pass,
No more are we glad of the joy of living,
   We see thro' a darkened glass,
For we've fought in the fields of Disillusion,
   And we are world-hardened—alas!

THE YEARS AND I.

We clasped our hands, the blithe young years and I,
We saw the luring world before us lie,
We laughed aloud, nor dreamed of tear and sigh,
We blessed our fate, the tide of hope ran high,
When we clasped hands, the blithe young years and I.

We saw love flit before us on the way,
And shine with light that far outshone the day,
We heard his call, we hastened to obey,
We sought him eagerly lest he'd delay
To show the site where his sweet city lay,
    The blithe young years and I.

We clasped our hands, the gray bent years and I,
We saw the darkened world behind us lie,
We wept aloud, we shook with sob and sigh,
We cursed our fate, the tide of grief ran high,
When we clasped hands, the gray bent years and I.

We saw death flit before us on the way,
And cast a shade that did obscure the day,
We heard his call, we trembled to obey,
We shrank from him as fain we would delay
To find the site where his dread city lay,
    The gray bent years and I.

THE POET'S SCORN.

I live in a land of fancy,—
   A land you know nothing of,
I smile in amazed derision
   At the common things you love.

I take the wings of wonder,
   And I sail to the edge of the world,
I see the mists of magic
   That round its rim are curled.

I hear sweet music waver,
   Then throb among the stars;
My spirit hears forever
   Those wondrous haunting bars.

I feel the flash and the glory
   Of a higher, nobler sphere,
And I thrill with passionate gladness
   That its bliss has found me here.

And you—you dream of the "markets,"
   Of "corners," night and morn,
So I smile at the range of your fancy,
   And fling you a poet's scorn!

THE LITTLE WOMAN.

Sweet little woman, two years old,
Cast in the Maker's daintiest mold,
Brightening my life with her sunny smiles,
Her coaxing ways and her baby wiles.
Busy—so busy with childish play,
But glad to creep to my arms and lay
Her little head on my happy breast,
While I crooned her into a dreamy rest ;
But what are these tears that my vision blur ?—
Ah ! the angels unbarred the gates for her,
Sweet little woman, two years old,
Cast in the Maker's daintiest mold !

Sweet little woman, two years old,
Safe with Christ on the streets of gold,
Watching for me by the Gates of Pearl,—
Dear little golden-haired baby girl !
Intently listening to hear the fall
Of my step as I answer the Saviour's call,
Ready to spring to my arms once more
As I moor my bark on the blessed shore.
So I patiently wait till the angel kind
Shall lead me where I am sure I'll find
The sweet little woman, two years old,
Safe with Christ on the streets of gold !

A MISCONCEPTION.

Love me? Nay now, defame not the word,
Love is the rarest thing on earth,
Rare as the fabled Phœnix bird
That finds in its death, a newer birth;
Burn up the ~~the~~ thing you call your love,
What life will arise from the ashes thereof?

Love me? Nay now, disgrace not the name,
Let not the bastard emotions you feel
Seek to share love's ineffable fame,
Or to fraudulent titles affix its seal.
A quivering lip, a kiss, a sigh—
These are the gauges you measure love by.

Love me? Nay now, you hardly have learned
The letters of love. Passion and Lust
Deeply their way in your being have burned,
And these you have christened Love and Trust,
A common error, few souls discern
The lack of *love* when *passions* burn.

GLADYS.

O the luminous eyes of sweet wide wonder,
    Gladys, my queen, my queen,
O the luscious lips of rich red ripeness,
    O the bronze hair's golden sheen!
How they roused my heart to riotous rapture,
    And stirred my blood like wine,
I had braved the perils of e'en Perdition
    To keep them forever mine!

O the heart that throbbed with a tender transport,
    Gladys, my queen, my queen,
Like the splendid bloom of a cactus flower
    Love's blush on the cheek, I ween!
O the subtle spell of the soul magnetic,
    Far-reaching and wild and free,
Like a meteor shod in a golden fire,
    It shot thro' the heart of me!

In the city of God's eternal quiet,
    Gladys, my queen, my queen,
On the dainty curves of the rounded bosom
    The gnawing death-worms lean!
The eyes are void, and the cheeks are hollow,
    The lips are a thin white thread,
The heart is mute in the desolate darkness,
    Gladys, my queen, is dead!

THE PESSIMIST'S VIEWS.

The world is a mighty fraud,
　　Nothing is as it seems,
Youth and truth and grace depart
　　Like evanescent dreams.
Nothing survives the test of years,
　　Love is a blissful cheat,
And when its heart grows old and cold,
　　It ceases to be so sweet.

Honor is but a name on earth,
　　A name all smutched with mire ;
Right is mostly governed by wrong,
　　And truth is often a liar.
The heart you lean on and love the best
　　Will be the first to fail,
The lips that give the closest kiss
　　Soonest begin to rail.

Beneath a smiling mask, dull Craft
　　Watches the chances of Fate,
He gorges in greed like a vampire bat
　　On the victims of his hate.
Nothing is done because it's right,
　　The question is still, what gain ?
Each in the race is for himself,
　　No matter what he may feign.

The apples of life are fair to see,
  They glow and redden in pride ;
But bite them once and you will find
  They're ashes and dust inside.
Treason and Error, Wrong and Hate,—
  These are the kings of earth ;
And Good that might usurp their crowns,
  Is strangled in its birth.

EVENTIDE.

'Tis eventide, and lo, we stand
Beside the misty border-land,
    My soul and I!
Upon the dim mysterious line
'Twixt Now and Then, we wait the sign
    That cuts the tie,
      My soul and I!

'Tis eventide, and lo, we wait
The swinging of the sealéd gate,
    My soul and I!
Our time-wrecked hopes come drifting near,
While to the world, a vain void sphere,
    We bid good-bye,
      My soul and I!

'Tis eventide, and lo, beyond
We think we see a beckoning hand,
    My soul and I!
We fix our eyes upon a star
Slow sailing to us from afar;
    To live we die,
      My soul and I!

THE WORLD'S DELUSIONS.

Roses that carry a canker,
    Crowns that cover a thorn,
Piercing with painful pressure
    The brows that they adorn.
These are the world's delusions,
    Deceits that we hold in scorn !

Sunlight that shapes a shadow,
    Gold that gildeth guile,
Triumphs that tell of toilings,
    Sighs that sting thro' a smile.
These are the world's delusions,
    Vanities void and vile.

Love that is sweet but shameful,
    Kisses that bless but bruise,
Passion that palls of pleasure,
    Delight that denies its dues.
These are the world's delusions,
    Dreams that its dreamers lose.

UNDER THE SOD.

Under the sod there is some one hiding,
   Hiding in a shroud ;
The roof of the house full close to the brows,
   Full close to the bosom proud!

Under the sod there is some one sleeping ;
   Sleeping safe and sound ;
In a gown of snow laid low, so low,
   And wrapped in silence round !

Under the sod there is some one dreaming,
   Dreaming hour on hour ;
For the night and the day are alike alway,
   Nor the suns nor the stars have power !

Under the sod there is some one lying,
   Lying unperplexed
By the tears and the toil and the strife for soil,
   Whereof the world is vexed !

Under the sod there is some one smiling,
   Smiling as a bride ;
For a love-knot ring the grave-worms cling,
   And for guests the ghosts abide !

THE CURSE OF RANK.

Behold me now, I am a prince of royal birth,
And coursing thro' my veins the proudest blood of earth
Proclaims my ancient line in pure and purple flow,
Heir to a throne am I, the mightiest below!
The haughty women of my house have mated kings,
Down crushing from their hearts love and its passionings!
And I, lo, even I must follow in their track
And smile the while my heart breaks for the love I lack!
The curse of rank! when young desire lays siege
To royal hearts, his death-knell this—*noblesse oblige!*
The curse of rank! that like a gulf impassible
Wide spreads 'twixt kings and fields where heavenly raptures dwell;
The curse of rank! that like a bitter blackened pall
Hides from kings' eyes alone the tenderest ties of all!
The curse of rank! that like an iron vice restrains
Kings' hearts, till they are as the veriest slaves in chains!
In secret, yea, in secret, we a little weep,
We kings of earth, a little hour a watch we keep
Beside the bier of love, a little space we sob
And curse in agony the empty pomps that rob
Us of our right to swoon in joy as other men
And keep the smiles of bliss beyond our longing ken.
I, heir apparent of the throne, I, royal prince,
Upon my wedding eve, I wail, I writhe, I wince
In passioned pain, for lo! the bride that waits my vow,
Within the chapel with her coroneted brow,

The Curse of Rank.

Is less to me than is the faintest memory of
The lowly maid of humble birth that won my love!
Ah me! when last I looked into her wide wet eyes
What passion uncontrollable I felt arise,
What fiery longing swept me like a whirlwind's breath
And made all else seem bitter to my soul save death.
Have I not often swathed me in her shadowy hair,
And ravaged with my kisses her round throat and fair,
And smiled to note the small red mark my sharp lips made?
Have we not both laughed low with love when close I laid
My clasp about her tender body to divine
Her heart beat stormily in unison with mine?
Have I not held her slender wrists, white as a flower,
And strong as steel in my warm grasp for hour on hour?
Have we twain not together drunk love's deepest springs?
My little woodland blossom! how my memory clings
About thee like an ivy vine—yea, tho' my bride
The daughter of a king, the chancel rail beside
My coming waits! O ye disastrous stars that rule
Kings' horoscopes, are we not puppet, yea, and fool
Of fate,—we whom the envious world account as great,
Hemmed in and hampered by our ceremonial state?
O ye three women blind who sit and spin the world,
What is the slavish spell ye have round princes curled?
What is this thing ye set upon their brows and call
A crown, that does but vex them as a grievous thrall?
Ah, to be free as other men! free from this rank,
Free from these royal chains that warningly do clank
Our obligations in our ears! But yesternight
Did I, prince of the realm, bowed down beneath the blight
Of blasted love, wander beside the sounding sea,

The Curse of Rank

And balance in my mind were it not gain to be
A straightened corpse, hid in the ocean's coral caves,
With sea-nymphs sobbing o'er me, and wild waves
A requiem chanting for my soul! To gratify
A code, the cravings of my heart must I deny!
Forevermore must I eschew the love of her,
My soft sweet blossom who alone hath power to stir
The heavy current of my heart! Nay, not for me
Must e'er again her tender pulse throb longingly—
A king's patrician line no common blood can cross,
A throne must mate a throne and love must bear the loss.
Adieu, sweet woodland blossom! at thy downy breast
No child of mine in blissful drowsiness will nest.
For mine but at the cost of virtue could'st thou be,
The curse of rank, belovêd one, parts thee and me!
Adieu! my bride awaits my coming, I must go
And vow the vows that seal me misery's slave. And lo!
The chattering world, base sycophant, will glibly prate
My royal happiness, the while I'm desolate!

A SONG OF DREAMS.

A dream of a merry child at play,
Blue eyed and fair, frolicsome, gay,
Glad as the birds in the Spring-time are,
Sorrows afloat like clouds afar,
Careless of trouble, untouched of fear,
Singing her way thro' the golden year.

A dream of a woman, old and gray,
Wrinkled and bent, wending her way
Lonesomely toward the last milestone
Where the grim dark shadow of death is thrown,
Storm-stained and weary and worn with care,
The candle of life at its final flare.

A dream of a grave in a churchyard lone,
Neglected, drear, with weeds o'ergrown,
With only the chirp of the cricket's song
As it sings in the grass the whole night long,
To break the silence that broods so deep,
Where the soul and the wornout body sleep.

THE RUSH OF THE TIMES.

SPIRIT.

What of the times, my brother ; how goes the world to-day,
Do men keep true and simple, have they still time to pray ?
And what of the Penates, the household gods, are they
Still loved and honored brother ; how goes the world to-day ?

MAN.

Alas ! the times are wicked,
   A curse is on the world,
The harpy of ambition
   Its wings has wide unfurled.
There's wrangling of the parties,
   There's battling for the spoils ;
The greed of power has bound men
   In slimy serpent coils.

There's brother fighting brother,
   And in the lust of gold,
As in the olden story,
   By his kin is Joseph sold.
No time have men for praying,
   " Lord ! Lord !" is all they say,
And alas for the Penates,
   With grimy dust they're gray !

The Rush of the Times.

The nations spit at nations,
    They plot, intrigue and plan,
Beneath the guise of treaty,
    How each may lead the van.
Man looks at man with doubting,
    The eyes of faith are blurred,
In every-day transactions
    Doubt is the carrion bird.

And no one trusts another,
    Each man is on his guard,
He ever fears betrayal,
    His heart is cold and hard.
The dead can scarce be buried,
    Ere like a lion's roar
Break curses from the living
    That they should gain no more.

No time—no time for praying,
    For meditation sweet,
It's a mighty rush and hurry
    For the temple's highest seat.
I fear me, oh, my brother,
    That men will lose their souls
In the mad desire for power
    That the present age controls.

SPIRIT.

Shame on your times, my brother; shame on your world to-day,
And shame on men and women that have no time to pray ;
Shame on their fevered folly, shame on their bloodless fray,
Shame on your times, my brother; shame on your world, I say.

FAREWELL.

Farewell, I leave you now for aye,
I will not come again. My way
Lies far apart from yours. No more
Will we keep pace upon the shore
Of Life and Love. The clock of Fate
Has tolled the hour to separate.
And yet one farewell kiss and sigh,
The last till in Death's arms we lie.

Across the bridge of broken dreams
I go into the realm that teems
With dead hopes; where the air is damp
With tears, and where the fire-fly's lamp
Lures to the dismal swamp of pain,
Where bleeding hearts are torn in twain,
And where the wild wind of regret
Like some Æolian harp that's set

Within a casement, wails in woe
Like tortured spirits damned below,
Into this desolation deep
I go alone. You cannot keep
Beside me there. Nor can your call
Pierce thro' the adamantine wall
Around the poisoned fen. My ear
Not e'en a cry from Heaven would hear.

Farewell.

Try not to follow me. Pass on
Your fated way. When I am gone
Some other love will comfort you,
And shed on life the roseate hue
Of re-born bliss. It is not meet
That you should grieve for me, my sweet.
Let me depart. I hear the knell
Rung from the bridge of dreams. Farewell.

THE STORY OF A SOUL.

I. WHICH?

Which wilt thou have, soul, song or love?
Wings of fancy that soar above
The stars themselves, or the maddening bliss,
The fiery rapture of love's close kiss;
The pale pure glories the poet knows,
Or the mute caresses passion bestows?
Which shall it be, soul, thou must choose
Which of the twain 'twere better to lose.

Which wilt thou have, soul, love or song?
The myriad marvels of dreams that throng
In the magical ether above the world,
Or the smile of lips that are softly curled?
A heart that throbs in tumultuous fashion,
Or cool, sweet peace untouched of passion?
Which shall it be, soul. Ponder thou,
For the burden of choice is on thee now!

Dream not that both can be thine, O soul,
One or the other from thee must roll
Love and its cup of delirious wine,
And the gift of song cannot both be thine.
No divided homage will either take,
The one must die for the other's sake.
Think of it, soul, and prayerfully,
The choice is for time and eternity.

II. THE SOUL'S CHOICE.

Came Love and Song unto me one day
(Thus the soul with a silver voice doth say),
And they stood with bated breath, each one,
Till my stormy struggles to choose were done.

Ah me! but Love, he looked fair and sweet,
O he flung a rich, red rose at my feet!
And he curved a smile on his laughing mouth,
And he sighed like a sweet spring wind from the South.

His mesmeric eyes were fixed upon mine—
O their glances thrilled me like maddening wine;
And I wellnigh forgot that Love dies in a day,
Such sorcery in his presence lay!

But there stood Song like a heavenly thing,
And a golden harp with many a string
He flung by the side of Love's red flower,
And its sweet notes fell in a vibrant shower.

And he showed me the Universe wide and vast,
And worlds of wonder came rolling past;
I gazed in his dreamy eyes, and saw
That the magic of Song must be my law.

So I chose me Song, and turned from Love
With a tear for the passionate joys thereof,
And the red rose paled in the dust and died,
But the harp's notes swelled with exultant pride!

III. THE SOUL'S REGRET.

By the pallid light of Life's last star,
I count what my gains and losses are,
And I feel, with an impotent dull despair,
That the pledges of Song were a subtle snare.

For one by one the strings of his lute
As the years crept by grew harsh or mute;
And the Universe wrapped itself in a cloud,
And the dreams fled fast in a frighted crowd.

And they left me alone and lonely where
The rim grows faint 'twixt the Here and the There;
And a wind swept out of the Past with a sigh,
And the wraith of Love sailed sadly by.

And the faint sweet scent of the crimson rose
That drooped and died on the day I chose
The Spirit of Song my guide to be,
Was borne on a breath of the wind to me.

And I stretched my arms with a vain desire,—
They but closed on a broken, silent lyre,—
I had made my choice for the gift of song
In the days gone by ; but I was awrong !

For Love and his one sweet passionate hour,
And his lustrous eyes and his blood-red flower,
Was a better thing than the empty show
Of the songs that failed—*too late I know !*

BABY.

Baby hands with waxen fingers,
In my soul their touch still lingers,
Baby hands in realms up higher
Twanging on a baby lyre.

Baby lips so warm and clinging,
Songs in glory now are singing,
Baby lips so sweetly smiling,
Saints in Heaven are now beguiling.

Baby eyes so shy and solemn,
Clearly my sad thoughts recall them,
Baby eyes from Eden peeping
Down to earth where I am weeping.

Baby feet so frail, unstable,
To walk unaided scarcely able,
Now in blest celestial regions
Walking with the happy legions.

Baby voice that sweetly stuttered
O'er the little prayers it uttered,
Now in Christ's great oratory
Lisping out its baby story.

Baby child, my life's one pleasure,
Loved beyond all earthly measure,
Now an angel held with favor
Closely to the loving Saviour.

PAOLO TO FRANCESCA.

Wert thou in Hell, Francesca,
  And I in Heaven, my love,
Thine eyes would be a magnet
  Would draw me from above.
The paly pallid glories
  Of saints would I disdain,
I'd fling me with mad rapture
  To share thy fiery pain.

Not all the hosts enransomed
  Could keep me from thy side;
Thou art my love, Francesca,
  Tho' Lanciotto's bride.
I'd find thee though God hid thee,
  I'd ferret thy retreat,
And I would make my Heaven
  In Hell with thee, my sweet!

ACROSS THE CROWD.

Across the crowd I met your eyes,
Across the dull short-sighted crowd,
And I alone by love made wise
Could see the tenderness arise,
And flash thro' cold convention's cloud !

Ah me ! but I was glad and proud
To muse upon our untold ties,
What time like common friends we bowed
          Across the crowd !

The dullards ! they could not surmise
How you enwrapped me with your eyes,
Nor penetrate the thin disguise ;
But I with keener sense endowed
Saw how to me your love-thoughts plowed
          Across the crowd !

DEAD.

A day and a night I've lain here dead,
Tapers burning at foot and head,
Jasmine, roses and eglantere
Lavishly scattered everywhere.
To think of it!   *Dead*, I've all these flowers,
I, who had none in my living hours,
All the years I've known since I was born,
No flower had I, but many a thorn!
'Tis often thus I've heard it said,
Thorns for the living and flowers for the dead!

They've closed the shutters and darked the room,
No light but the tapers' breaks the gloom,
And to stir the still there's but the clock
With its everlasting " tick, tick, tock."
The children at times, with awed, scared faces
Peep at me here in my flowers and laces,
And then creep out with stealthy tread,
Afraid of me, now I am lying dead!

They brought the baby awhile ago,
I almost started to hear him crow,
It struck as loud on the silent air
As a clarion call had echoed there.
When they touched his hand to my frozen brow
I nearly smiled to notice how
He started back with a wailing cry,
And turned from me with a fearful eye.

Dead.

It seems so strange to have naught to do—
I, whose labor was never thro',
I, who toiled for years and years,
Lying with eyelids too quiet for tears,
And hands that so seldom were at rest,
Crossed in idleness on my breast!

There's plenty to do down stairs, I know,
I can fancy them hurrying to and fro;
When I think how terribly tired they'll be,
Now that they have no help from me,
I feel almost as it were a sin
To be set apart from the work and the din;
But oh, the *rest* to be lying dead,
With the tapers burning at foot and head!

YEARNING.

O heart unsatisfied !
What is it in the mighty wide
Infinitude that thou dost crave ?
The stars that climb upon the night
And sail the skies like ships of light ?
Between them and thee lies a grave !
Thou canst not woo them to thy side,
    O heart unsatisfied!

O heart unsatisfied !
What passionate desires denied,
What yearning for a hopeless height,
What vain out-reachings of despair,
What claspings but of viewless air,
What phantoms mock thee in their flight
That thou wouldst have with thee abide,
    O heart unsatisfied !

SWEETHEART.

Sweetheart's hair was a golden shower,
Sweetheart's brow was a snow white flower,
Sweetheart's cheeks were pink as the roses
Where the flush of love on their leaves reposes.

Sweetheart's eyes were the purple pansies
Brimming over with soulful fancies;
Sweetheart's lips were the ripe red cherries
Where the smile of the sun the longest tarries.

Sweetheart's hands were carven marble,
Sweetheart's song was a bird-like warble,
Sweetheart's voice was the purling waters,
Sweetheart—the fairest of earth's fair daughters.

Sweetheart's throat was a white narcissus,
Her breath like the sweet spring winds that kiss us,
Sweetheart's thoughts were purer than heaven,
Freer than saints' from worldly leaven.

Sweetheart's soul is a soul in glory,
Done on the earth is Sweetheart's story,
In paradise were the angels lonely,
They yearned for Sweetheart and Sweetheart only.

Sweetheart peers o'er the walls of jasper,
Sweetheart smiles when I strive to clasp her,
Death's rolling river I must first cross over,
Ere my loved, lost Sweetheart I recover.

PROGRESS.

Whate'er the morbid doubters say,
The world grows better day by day,
   The liberal arts have wider scope,
   The stars that rule earth's horoscope
The march of Progress now betray.

Old superstitions have decayed,
The waves of truth erstwhile delayed
   Are flooding o'er the people's ranks,
   And men are treading solid planks
By Righteousness and Reason laid.

Adown the vista of the years
The light of Liberty appears,
   At first a flickering gleam afar,
   But now, ablaze like some great star,
She shines the chief of radiant spheres.

The slavish bonds that nations curst,
The patriot's power has long since burst,
   Freedom's hallelujahs rise
   Till e'en the stars laugh in the skies—
Oppression's march has been reversed.

Fanatic dogmas, canons, creeds,
The soul enfranchised no more heeds,
   No set devotion is compelled,
   The hand of Tolerance is upheld,
And each man worships as he needs.

Progress.

The stately ship of Knowledge rolls
In every port where eager souls
   Wait anxiously her precious freight,
   For all the lowly as the great,
The knell of Ignorance she tolls.

Whene'er a bold strong spirit dares
Uplift the veil Creation wears,
   On his head she gladly lays
   Crowns of laurel and of bays,
And his triumph proudly shares.

One by one the lawless ways
Of the old barbarian days
   Down Disuse's vault are cast;
   From the shadow of the Past
The Present climbs to nobler praise.

Yea, the world is wiser, better,
Every day she casts some fetter,
   Onward lies her path, and higher,
   To Perfection's goal she's nigher,
Both in spirit and in letter.

IN DIALECT.

HIDE FRAE THE WORLD.

Wide the world, darlings,
   Sair are its stings,
Swaddled in shadows
   The blessings it brings ;
Then heed not the fletherin'
   Sangs that it sings,
But close cuddle under
   Your mither's warm wings.

Low'rin' the lift, dears,
   Above it that's curled,
Painful the pitfalls
   Whare you may be hurled ;
Then nestle contented
   Wi' frail pinions furled,
And tempt not its terrors—
   Oh, hide frae the world !

WHEN THE FIERCE FATES FROWN!

One by one frae the auld hame-nest
   The birdies flit awa',
One by one frae the mither's breast
   The bairnies turn them a'.

One by one when the night draps down
   Seek the birds the nestward track;
One by one when the fierce fates frown
   Steal the sorrowing bairnies back.

MY LADDIE.

There is a lad I lo'e sae dear,
    Heigh ho, my laddie O !
He wears nae grand nor gaudy gear,
He has nae leesome lands, I fear,
But still I lo'e him, oh sae dear,
    Heigh ho, my laddie O !

He has a laughin' eye o' of blue,
    Heigh ho, my laddie O !
His mou's a red rose wat wi' dew,
O aftentimes he pressed it to
My ain till ae our twa' mou's grew,
    Heigh ho, my laddie O !

Like yellow gowd his silk hair is,
    Heigh ho, my laddie O !
Braw gowd the sunshine lo'es to kiss—
(I'm mickle like the sun i' this !)
My breastie weel nigh bursts wi' bliss,
    Heigh ho, my laddie O !

Let them wha' will choose wealth and power,
    Heigh ho, my laddie O !
Withouten love they both will sour,
I wadna swap wi' them an hour,
My laddie's smile's a richer dower,
    Heigh ho, my laddie O !

PARTED.

The simmer is sae green, my love,
The skies are liquid blue above,
The birdies warble i' the trees
And croon the sweetest lullabies,
But naething a' these are to me
Sin' I am far, my love, frae thee.

The glaizie sunlight fa's sae soft,
The win's the rose's sweetness waft,
The purlin' river wimples by,
A mirror for the sinny sky;
But nane o' these can gladden me
Sin' I am far, my love, frae thee.

The lee-lang day I sit my lane
Wi' heart as heavy as a stane,
The smilin' features o' the day
Can drive nane o' my tears away,
Ilk sight and sound is sad to me
Sin' I am far, my love, frae thee.

SAE ILL THE DAY!

O, I hae gi'en my heart away,
Sae ill the day, sae ill the day!
I see na mair the sun and moon
Nor a' the twinklin' stars aboon,
I onie see twa een o' blue
Wi' sparks o' sunlight shootin' thro'.

O, I hae gi'en my heart away,
Sae ill the day, say ill the day!
I hear na mair the lintwhite's sang,
Nor ither birds wha lilt alang,
I onie hear a siller voice
Whase echo makes my saul rejoice.

O, I hae gi'en my heart away,
Sae ill the day, sae ill the day!
I wad it were my ain again,
For fickle is the love o' men.
I aften think o' ane I fear
Wha lang has ceased to haud me dear.

O, I hae gi'en my heart away,
Sae ill the day, sae ill the day!
I sleep na mair a quiet sleep
When silence broods sae black and deep,
I onie lie awake and greet
That love has proven bitter-sweet!

THE CHIMLA-LUG.

I sit beside the chimla-lug,
Adrinkin' o' the cheerin' mug,
A cantie lad I am and braw,
I care na' for the warld at a'.

I sit beside the chimla-lug,
Adrinkin' o' the cheerin' mug,
It's hame-brewed ale alane that's guid
To fire the heart and warm the bluid.

I sit beside the chimla-lug,
Adrinkin' o' the cheerin' mug,
I toss a health to them I lo'e,
May they misfortune never know.

I sit beside the chimla-lug,
Adrinkin' o' the cheerin' mug,
A cantie lad I am and braw,
I care na' for the warld at a'.

THE BAIRNS.

It's the bonnie wee bairns we a' o' us lo'e,
The bonnie wee bairns wi' sauls like the snow,
The dainty wee bairns, the sonsie wee bairns,
The wee bits o' bairns wha sweeten our woe.

It's the bonnie wee bairns we a' haud sae dear,
The bonnie wee bairns wha bring us sic cheer,
The dainty wee bairns, the sonsie wee bairns,
The wee bits o' bairns warth a' the warld's gear.

It's the bonnie wee bairns for wham we wad die,
The bonnie wee bairns sae cunnin' and sly,
The dainty wee bairns, the sonsie wee bairns,
The wee bits o' bairns wha' drapt frae the sky.

SCOTCH SONG.

Your een are like a dusky sky,
Whare drownéd twa stars smilin' lie,
The rosy blossom o' your mou'
Wad tempt a bee for hiney-dew.

Your brow's a snaw-drap, pure and proud,
Set in a crown o' curlin' gowd,
And in your chin a dimple is,
Whare Cupid cleft it wi' a kiss.

Sae jimp your waist that I could span
It amaist wi' one brawnie han',
And when your gracefu' form I see
I'm minded o' the hazel-tree.

But 'tis na for your charms o' face,
Nor for your souple lissome grace,
That I hae tint my heart to you,
But 'tis because your saul is true.

ALANE.

Alane beside the chimla-cheek,
Wi' heart sae fu' I canna' speak,
For lang syne days I sit and greet,
Till a' the warl' swims i' the weet.

Alane beside the chimla-cheek,
I sit and watch the curlin' reek,
Until I see thro' mists o' tears
The faces loved in ither years.

Alane beside the chimla-cheek—
O fleetin' human ties sae weak!
O load o' life sae hard to bear
When dear ones sit wi' us na mair!

MIRANDY.

Of all the cur'us and wonderful capers!
Mirandy hez took to writin' fer papers!
It's 'mazin' the larnin' Mirandy hez,
I trem'le sometimes at the big words she sez.
We sent her to school, her mother and me,
And now she's come back as larned as kin be.
She kin talk 'bout books till yer head'll spin round,
And her equal in figgers they say can't be found.

And now jes' to think of the pome that she's writ,
With nary a soul to help her a bit.
I allers said she'd a look in her eye
As showed she wuz cut out for somepin more high
Nor the rest of us wuz. You'd be stunned to hear
The piece that she's writ. I can't be quite clear
What it is she's ameanin', but that ain't no harm,
Fer she larfed when I told her and said that the charm

Of po'try lay in concealin' the thought,
And that wuz the only kind that wuz bought.
Well, p'rhaps that suits scholars, but jes' here atween us,
I kin tell you I don't think I 'preciate genius.
I'd fur ruther read what the news is from town
Than the wonderfullest pome that wuz ever writ down.
The hymn-book I like some, and Baxter's Saints' Rest,
But the Bible's the readin' that I love the best.

Mirandy.

But Mirandy is different and so is her ma,
Sech a change in that woman you never have saw.
She wants to be larned as Mirandy she does.
Sence the pome wuz writ the like never wuz!
She uses the same high falutin' grand talk,
And I stare at her jes' like a big, stupid gawk.
Half the time I don't know what on eirth she kin mean,
And I hate to be larfed at as ef I wuz green.

I'm proud of 'em both tho'—their larnin' is fine,
And in kumpany I feel some like it wuz mine.
I'm a leetle afraid of Mirandy, I am,
Tho' to look at she's jes' as mild as a lamb.
But somehow she seems kinder fur off to me
And not quite the same as she ust to be
Afore she took to cuttin' sech capers
As writin' strange pomes fer the daily papers!

WRAPPED UP IN LITERATOOR.

This is a ill that yarbs can't cure,
To be jes' wrapped up in literatoor,
My gal Mirandy took to it once,
But I'd fur ruther she'd stayed a dunce.

Commonplace ways she can't enjure
Sence she got wrapped up in literatoor.
She gits worser and worser with every day,
And she's actooally took to rhymin' fer pay.

Strange what folks kin see in sech things,
Mirandy, she says it's the Muse that sings—
(That's somepin them pome-makers tries to allure
When they git wrapped up in literatoor).

I wrote 'bout Mirandy once afore,
The time when she first began to "soar,"
Then she hadn't the fever so bad, I'm sure,
But *now* she's wrapped up in literatoor.

Rhymin' and writin' and burnin' the ile
So late that I'm sure her complexion 'll spile,
I wisht to goodness there was some cure
Fer gittin' wrapped up in literatoor.

ns.

INVOCATION TO TIME.

Rock me to patience, Time, lull me to rest,
Hold me in tenderness close to thy breast;
Say me some prayer, Time, sing me some song,
Drown in thy melodies memories of wrong.
Soothe me with touches, Time, tell me thy beads,
Pour on my spirit the comfort it needs.
Teach me thy spell, Time, show me thy charm,
Guard me forever from danger and harm.
Lend me thy staff, Time, stay my faint feet,
Lead me in vales ever blooming and sweet!

HAPPY.

On her bridal morn, in her bridal dress,
She smiled transfigured by happiness.
The sun sailed high in a cloudless sky,
And the sweet soft winds of love swept by,
Whispering low as they kissed this one,
"Happy is the bride that the sun shines on."

O the years and the years! how they roll them away!
How they bring her e'en to the burial day.
O the rhythmic beat of the rain's soft feet,
How it soothes the dead in her slumber sweet;
How it whispers low, "This is blessedness won,
Happy is the corpse that the rain rains on."

COVER THE EMBERS.

Cover the embers ! love is a-dying !
Wan on the hearth of the heart it is lying.
    Passion a-paling,
    Fire a-failing,
Mists of Oblivion over it sailing !

Cover the embers ! love is a-dying !
Hist to the gravewind a-sobbing and sighing,
    Cypresses trailing,
    Dole bells a-wailing,
Ashes of memories the last glimmers veiling!

A BREAK IN THE CIRCLE.

(TO MY SISTER.)

Out of the old home into the new,—
With a smiling sigh and a tear or two,
And haunting memories not a few,
We pray, while the world wears a misty hue,
Now and forever be God with you !

Out of the old home into the new—
With a tremulous laugh that rings untrue,
And lashes wet with a tender dew,
We pray, while you seem to swim in our view,
Now and forever be God with you !

ONLY A MEMORY.

We know by the winds that are sadly sighing,
The fair fond summer is fleetly flying ;
We know by the ruinous wrecks of the clover,
The swooning sweet of the year is over !

We know by the middle-skies, scant of fire,
The sun is aweary of climbing higher ;
We know by the woodland of russet-red splendor,
The summer is only a memory tender !

THUS IT IS.

A little bitter and a little sweet ;
    Thus it is that the world runs on.
A cross to carry and a crown to meet,
Lilies of love, and a winding sheet ;
    Thus it is that the world runs on.

A little bliss and a little pain ;
    Thus it is that the world runs on.
A shaft of sunshine and a shower of rain,
A burial crowding a bridal train ;
    Thus it is that the world runs on.

JUNE.

When June was the queen of the year's desire,
   And the days were a dream of love,
The sun like a ship of molten fire,
   Sailed the infinite ocean above.

The fair fresh hills in their emerald glory
   Rivalled the rarest gem,
The roses blushed at the ardent story,
   The soft winds whispered to them.

With a limped languor, the rippling river
   Lazily lilted along,
And the birds, sweet gifts of a Gracious Giver,
   Warbled a bridal song.

LOVE'S SANCTITY.

Love ! lightly to our lips full often springs
That word of Christ's divinest utterings.
We say it easily, with flippant tongue,
That power by which the starry spheres were swung
In Heaven ; that mighty agony for which
A God was crucified, a world to rich !

Love ! circle round the word a flaming fire
That none but God-like souls may e'er aspire
To name its name ! Let puny wordlings blush
To dare intrude their babblings on its hush,
Let them learn to forego their idle prate
And keep Love's sanctity inviolate !

LULLABYE.

Winsome wee baby so fast asleep,
    Lullabye, lullabye, babe !
Stars like the eyes of angels peep
Out of the heavens a watch to keep,
Winsome wee baby so fast asleep,
    Lullabye, lullabye, babe !

Winsome wee baby asleep in God,
    Lullabye, lullabye, babe !
Daisies and violets softly nod,
Startling up from the burial sod,
Winsome wee baby asleep in God,
    Lullabye, lullabye, babe !

THOU AND I.

Thou and I in the life-flush, sweet,
Buds and blossoms and fervid heat,
Song and laughter and close caress,
Infinite love and tenderness,
Naught in the world but blissful youth,
Death but a far off dream in sooth.

Thou and I in the graveyard, sweet,
Creeping ivy from head to feet,
Silence eternal and deep laid rest,
The death-worm close to each frozen breast,
Left of us, and our passionate trust,
Frightsome bones and loathsome dust!

SUNSET.

The west was a sea of splendor,
   The sun a fiery boat,
The clouds were flame-tipped billows,
   The hills, red worlds remote.

The west was a sombre ocean,
   The sun a ship gone down,
The clouds were wild gray breakers,
   The hills a shadowed town.

ECHOES.

O silvery echoes blown from yesterday,
    Ye do repeat
    Some notes so sweet,
I'd have ye echo in my life for aye,
And never in the silence die away,
O silvery echoes blown from yesterday!

O silvery echoes blown from yesterday,
    Ye do recall
    A vanished thrall,
Ye do remind me of Love's laureled May,
Reverberate forever here, I pray,
O silvery echoes blown from yesterday!

LIBERTY.

What form is this comes marching down
Like a streak of light thro' the aisles of Time,
Wearing proudly a glittering crown,
By story heralded and song and rhyme,
Scattering darkness and spreading the light,
Hailed with thunders of wild delight?

'Tis the matchless form of *Liberty*, grand;
See how the nations wheel into line,
And one by one kiss her beckoning hand;
See the halo of glory around her shine,
As she stands in the fane like a heavenly vision,
With her foot on the brow of dead Oppression.

THE VOICELESS.

"Only the voiceless speak forever."—Ingersoll on Conkling

The dwellers who dwell in the Silent City,
   Where the waves of Sound are never stirred ;
They whose muteness the foolish pity,
   They are the speakers eternally heard.

"Only the voiceless speak forever ! "
   Their silent language is heard by all ;
The ears of the heart and the soul heed ever
   The words of the dead as a trumpet call !

The voiceless ! the words that they breathe are immortal !
   Their eloquent echoes resound thro' the earth,
Of the silence that lies at the grave's solemn portal
   The noblest of languages daily has birth !

YEA!

Yea! childhood wept!
    For trifling toys,
    For babyish joys,
    But life was bright,
    And grief was light,
When childhood wept!

Yea! girlhood wept!
    For lost illusions,
    Love's delusions,
    Yet still the sun
    Had hours to run,
When girlhood wept!

Yea! womanhood wept!
    Such bitter tears,
    For sweet lost years;
    All other grief
    Was small and brief,
When womanhood wept!

SIRIUS.

I watched the darkling dome of night
Grow flecked with God's eternal eyes,
With pulsing heart and ravished sight
I saw great Sirius arise.

Like to a king of royal state
Swept he in splendor to his throne.
The stars paid tribute, small and great,
When Sirius the Dog-star shone.

The moon, an orb of argent fire,
Crept out, and turned her face amazed
To where, as tho' he would out-vie her,
Bold Sirius in brilliance blazed.

SHADOWED.

Where the rose blooms there is the canker;
In the fertile soul the weeds grows ranker;
There are graves in the beautiful sea;
Sweet is the wine, but bitter the lees;
The winds that freshen can spread disease;
There's a sting in the honey-bee.

No good, but an ill beside it grows;
No light but some darkening shadow knows;
No sweet but some bitter affords;
No joy but some pain is also there;
Hope is companioned by chill despair;
Even Eden is shadowed by swords.

FIRST AND LAST.

The first sweet passionate kiss of love!
Divinity drawn from heaven above,
Nectar the gods grow drunk upon,
Magic that whirls new worlds to dawn!

The last sad passionate kiss of love!
Despair and the deep desolation thereof,
Hemlock that steals the fire of breath,
Shadow that sweeps old worlds to death!

SWEET YESTERDAY.

Dead and buried and in its grave,
    Yesterday, sweet yesterday!
Ah, but its smile was bright and brave,
And a passionate pleasure its moments gave,
    Yesterday, sweet yesterday!

In its winding-sheet this many an hour,
    Yesterday, sweet yesterday!
Only a thing the worms devour
And divide as they do some dear dead flower
    Yesterday, sweet yesterday!

BITTER SWEET.

Love has sweets and honeyed smiles,
    But love has salty tears ;
The dauntless heart of love beguiles
    Into the realm of fears.

Love has laughs and crimson lips,
    But love has mournful eyes ;
The voice of love lures lonely ships
    Where song in silence dies.

Love has blessings, blissful dreams,
    But love has curses too ;
Beware of love, he fairest seems
    When he has least for you.

The Daisy.

THE DAISY.

Hark! 'tis the June that I hear to-day!
She leans her lips to the earth to say,
"There are stars in the skies, but I love the best
The starry daisies upon thy breast!"

And the brave earth breathes in the ear of June,
While the wild birds chant a lilting tune,
"There are fairer flowers and buds more bold,
But the daisy's heart is a heart of gold!"

LO! WHEN THE MOON.

Lo ! when the moon in full-orbed splendor sailed
      Across the night,
The farther stars before her beauty paled
      And hid their light.

One large, low rebel, bolder than the rest
      In Heaven's mild main,
His signal set, and followed unsuppressed
      Fast in her train.

The field of fleecy clouds that dared presume
      To veil her face,
In silence swept to white impassioned doom,
      Blanched by her grace.

THE HERITAGE.

What was hid in the heart of the years?
The husks of life and sharp salt tears !
What winds were blown from the hills of love?
Sad winds that died with a mournful sough !
What heritage to the soul is given?
A grave on earth—and the fable—Heaven !

THE CROWNING OF GENIUS.

Genius stood up in the fane to be crowned—
All the nations of earth came thither to see,
Fair Innocence ringed him and danced around,
And orchestral music swelled wild and free.
Brave knights in armor, and ladies grand
Sued humbly each for a touch of his hand.

The lanterns swung high like living things,
The incense burned in a censer of gold,
There was heard the flutter of unseen wings,
When chanting priests in white robes stoled
Placed on his head the Thing they bore—
And lo!' twas a crown of thorns he wore!"

THE END.

www.ingramcontent.com/pod-product-compliance
Lightning Source LLC
Chambersburg PA
CBHW020129170426
43199CB00010B/697